Home In All Seasons

The Clifton Community Woman's Club
Clifton, Virginia

© 2024

All rights reserved. No part of this book may be reproduced in any form whatsoever, without the written permission of the author, or the Clifton Community Woman's Club.

ISBN 9798325266706

Dedication

This work is dedicated to the Clifton Community and to those who work tirelessly to improve the lives of others.

May we each find beauty in all seasons.

Winter . . .

Spring . . .

Summer . . .

Autumn . . .

Home
In All Seasons

A compilation of Photographs

Homes and Descriptions
Floral Arrangements
Ideas, Tips, and Recipes

The Clifton Community Woman's Club

Table of Contents

Preface xv

Chapter One – Winter 1
- The Zimmerman Home, winter photograph 3
- The Holidays 4
- The Cranston Home, winter photograph 15
- Focal Points and Salvaged Treasures 16
- Tips 25
- Holiday History – Valentine's Day 29
- Simple Recipes to warm your heart when the weather outside is frightful! 31

Chapter Two – Spring 34
- The Cranston Home on Tour 35
- Spring Flowers Gathered from the Garden 38
- The Whiteside Home at Easter 44
- Holiday History-Why Bunnies and Eggs at Easter? 49
- Create Beautiful Tables 52
- Harmonize Color 57
- Create Beautiful Dishes, too! 61
- More Tempting Spring Treats 65

Chapter Three – Summer 68
- The Zimmerman Home on Tour 70
- Welcoming Entrances 82
- Cool Summer Whites 90
- The Luchini Great Room 95
- Tip: Think Outside the Vase 102
- The Charneco Addition 106
- Summer Birthdays? 114
- The Tastes of Summer – Cool and fresh or a little spicy 115

Chapter Four – Autumn 118
   The Wood Home on Tour 120
   The Colors of Autumn 140
   Holiday History – Halloween Happenings 146
   Festive Décor 153
   Holiday History – Thanksgiving 159
   The Flavors of Fall 162
   Home in all seasons – The Neckels' Gazebo 167

Chapter Five – Retirement Community Living . . . 171
   The Gilbert Home 173
   The Kershenstein Home 176
   Tip: Create a Vignette 179
   The Post Home 180
   The Smith Home 185

Chapter Six – CCWC - What We Do 187
   CCWC Beginnings – Diane Smith 188
   Programs and Committees 189
   The Lamb Center – Karen Kershenstein 190
   Scholarships – Barbara Keller 192
   Environment Committee Tips – Vickie Luchini . . . 193
      Going Green with Gold – Peggy Cranston . 195

Appendix – Sponsors 197
Credits/Contributors 198
Recipe for Salt Dough Ornaments 199

About the Authors – the CCWC Membership 201
Make a House a Home – from Peter Townsends' Irish
   Blessings 202

Preface

The Clifton Community Woman's Club

The CCWC was founded over 50 years ago to promote friendships and to serve the community through activities and projects that enhance the cultural, educational, and physical well-being of the community. Our Charitable Trust contributes thousands of dollars to other charitable organizations, mostly local, and towards scholarships at George Mason University and Northern Virginia Community College. An additional scholarship is awarded annually to a local high school senior. The high school rotates each year.

We'd like to thank those who have contributed photographs of their homes for this book. In these pages you will see decorated spaces, welcoming niches, a tip or two, and beautiful floral arrangements created by CCWC members - even some seasonal recipes to whet your appetite. Perhaps these photos will inspire your own creativity. We are grateful to those who generously contribute their time and treasure to support our efforts. Please see a more complete list of our sponsors and contributors in the Appendix.

The Zimmermans' Clifton Home in Winter

The Holidays

This front door says welcome all season with evergreens and a sprig of Firepower Nandina.

The warm glow within is so inviting, especially during the holidays when family and friends gather together.

Festive Tables

The Luchini family's traditional holiday table is covered in a Tartan Plaid wool cloth and a red lace runner, and is set with Christmas china and Ruby glass. Napkins were folded by this homeowner into Elf booties! The beautiful English Windsor chairs are two hundred years old.

The Cranston dining room table is also dressed for the holidays with boxwood topiaries, brass horns, and candles. More boxwood greenery is tucked into the crystal chandelier above the table. The mirror has been hanging over the mahogany buffet, both circa 1940, for over 80 years! First, in the childhood home of Mrs. Cranston, and now many moves later, they grace this dining room.

The Paris family enjoys entertaining, and as you will see in coming seasons, they lavishly decorate for all holidays.

The Portland family also enjoys entertaining, especially at Christmas. Family and friends are frequently gathered around their table set with holiday dishes on a Belgian Lace cloth from Mrs. Portland's travels to Bruges in 1988.

Over the buffet in their dining room on the wall opposite the fireplace hang two framed pieces of cloth – protected heirlooms – beautifully displayed. Mrs. Portland cannot remember the type of needlework they are except Drawn Thread

Linen, which she found on You Tube; but she did share a little of their story. The curtains are

about 90 years old. Mrs. Portland's mother brought them in her Trousseau Chest when she came to the United States. They were a gift from an aunt for her marriage in 1932. She had planned to put them on a window in her new country; however, the windows in the US were too large and she just put them away.

Her mother gave them to her when the Portlands moved to Virginia. Mrs. Portland tried to just hang them on the wall but decided to have them framed instead. After her father died, her mother would come and stay with them during the winter and summer. She would often stop and look at them with a smile. She would say that they brought back many memories.

Mrs. Portland's parents were born in the Tyrol, the south Alps of Austria. After World War One, the area was taken by Italy for a pass through the Alps to reach other countries. When asked of her parents where they were born, they always answered that they came from the Alps in Northern Italy, the Tyrol. They held on to their heritage all through their lives.

The Portlands mantels in the dining room and den are decorated with handmade pinecone wreaths, purchased at a Christmas Bazaar 40 years ago.

Mantels are a great place to welcome every season. The wreaths over the mantel above were handmade by the homeowner from grapevines on their property, made originally for her daughter's wedding.

The Cranston Home in Winter

Clifton, Virginia

Focal Points and Salvaged Treasures

The fireplace is the focal point of the Cranstons' living room.

An impressive focal point of the Esser family's great room is this massive fireplace constructed of Bluestone rocks quarried in Albermarle, Virginia, seen on the opposite page. It is a Count Rumford designed fireplace, commonly built in the early 1800s. It has a tall opening, a shallow fire box and angled sides which reflect more heat into a room. The candelabra on the hearth stood for many years at the altar in an old Michigan church, and the mantel is made from the remains of a Kentucky log cabin.

The Essers added many unique features and thoughtful touches to their contemporary Clifton home, completed in 1981. It is constructed of Virginia Bluestone and California Redwood, symbolically uniting the east and west. They have shared more of their treasured finds from other parts of the US on the following pages.

The Esser family salvaged old stained-glass windows from Victorian homes that had been razed in St. Louis, Missouri. They brought them to Virginia to incorporate into their new home. One went in their new barn! Another – over the tub in a second floor bathroom. A third is displayed in a grouping on the wall, and a fourth is part of a window on the first floor.

The stained-glass window on the following page was salvaged out of that same old church in Michigan where the candelabra was found. To think, the beautiful round window, now above the Essers' staircase, once shone down on parishioners in a small Michigan town; while the candelabra, now on their hearth in the great room, lit their faces at the altar.

This ceiling medallion and light fixture was taken out of an old demolished 1900s home in St. Louis and now hangs in the Essers' dining room. The light was made during the transition time from gas home lighting to electricity, and this light was made with both capabilities... gas and electricity. The Essers had the gas portion of the old fixture wired for electricity when it was installed.

So many unique features in their home.

Saddle up to the bar! Definitely a focal point of the Essers' lower level entertainment room. The front panel of the bar is made from an old Saint Charles, Missouri courthouse chamber door.

Opposite the hanging horse bits are Longhorns from Texas. The Esser family had horses for many years and were avid riders. The room has a definite western vibe. Perfect for parties!

Tip: Show off your special ornaments . . .

The Portlands hang some of their favorite Christmas balls on ribbons from the ceiling, intriguing their guests. They bring back fond memories of their 62 years of marriage!

Tip: A novel way to display White House ornaments . . .

The Portlands have been collecting White House Ornaments since 1983, two years before moving to their current Fairfax home. Mrs. Portland started displaying the ornaments on ribbons to hang on the sides of open doorways of the dining room, and she now has seven ribbons with almost six ornaments per ribbon. They are still collecting.

Tip: Spray some branches with white paint and glue on mirror tiles (found in any craft store) to give an arrangement an extra sparkle and a wintry feel.

Tip: When you need to have several centerpieces or arrangements that are alike, wrap boxes in the same paper, insert any container - a can, jar, etc. - and tie with pretty ribbon. Natural Kraft paper works, too, and is inexpensive.

Valentine's Day

Many of our celebrations and holidays have pagan roots. Valentine's Day may have had its origin in a pagan fertility festival that was celebrated in early Rome in mid February. The festival was outlawed in the 5th century, when around this time, the Pope declared February 14th St. Valentine's Day, named for a martyred priest.

As the stories go, there were two men named Valentine who were executed on February 14th in different years by Emperor Claudius II. One of these priests was imprisoned for secretly officiating at wedding ceremonies for Roman soldiers, as it was against the law for soldiers to marry. The other was believed to have fallen in love with a young girl while in prison. He began writing to her, and before his death, he sent her a letter signed, "From your Valentine."

In Shakespeare's time love letters were exchanged to celebrate the day. However, it was in the mid 19th century and the Victorian Era that many of our current day practices became widely popular – chocolates, flowers, and cards. The phrase, "From your Valentine," is still a popular phrase today.

Since Roman times the rose has been a symbol of love, but it was not given as a gift for Valentine's Day until the Victorian Era.

Simple Recipes to warm your heart when the weather outside is frightful!

SIMPLE SALMON

1 lb. Salmon filet
½ c. sliced green onions (both white and green parts)

Marinade:
¼ c. soy sauce
¼ c. olive oil
¼ c. lemon juice

Combine marinade ingredients in a plastic bag. Once combined, add salmon and refrigerate for up to an hour. Pan sauté for 5 minutes on each side over medium to medium high heat for medium doneness. Discard marinade in bag.
Once salmon is cooked, sprinkle the top with the green onions. Serves 2 or 3.

FIVE-CUP SALAD

1 c. mandarin oranges
1 c. pineapple chunks (canned, drained)
1 c. sour cream
1 c. sweetened shredded coconut
1 c. miniature marshmallows

Need more color for the Christmas holidays? Add a ½+ cup of chopped maraschino cherries. Gently stir all ingredients and chill for at least 2 hours. Serves 4.

OOEY GOOEY CAKE

Cake: 1 box yellow cake mix
            ½ c. butter, melted
            1 egg, slightly beaten

Topping: 1-8 oz. package cream cheese, room temperature
              2 eggs, slightly beaten
              2 ¾ c. powdered sugar

Heavily grease a 9 X 13 baking dish. In the pan, mix only cake ingredients to moisten. Mix together until smooth: cream cheese, eggs and powdered sugar. Pour over basic cake in pan leaving about ½" of the edge exposed. Bake for 30-40 minutes at 350 degrees. Cool and cut into squares. (It is more a cookie bar recipe than a cake.)

Note: This is a very misunderstood dessert that has won many baking contests. It's so easy and tasty.

All so easy and good in any season!

Chapter Two

Spring

The Cranstons designed their retirement home with wide hallways and graceful arches. It was completed in December, 2003. The dianthus are in bloom in early May and make a colorful carpet to welcome friends and family. Peonies, just in front of the yellow-green mops in the foreground, will be opening soon. Those will be followed by late blooming azaleas just behind the dianthus . . . Planned for color in every season.

As you enter the home, double archways lead from the foyer into the spacious living room on the right. French doors from the living room open onto a screened porch and a deck beyond.

The screened porch is a three season retreat for this family. The floor was hand-painted by the homeowner. The pattern echoes the foyer.

Fresh lemon slices in a tall vase with yarrow, greens, and trailing ivy just say spring . . . and summer, too!

Spring Flowers Gathered from the Garden

Early Spring Hellebores – in a teapot

Late Spring Peonies

. . . high and low

Astilbe and Princess Spirea supported with pebbles

And all beautifully arranged.

The Autons' garden has been a source of peonies for CCWC Homes' Tours for many years. Several of the arrangements seen in this book contain peonies from their garden.

Fresh flowers on a handmade cross or Easter bunnies on your door – both say welcome and . . .

As you enter the Whitesides' Fairfax home, you are welcomed with bunnies – bunnies on the door, in the windows, snuggled on many of the beautiful antique pieces that fill the interior.

The old English bar, pictured here, was found by the homeowners on one of their many antiquing excursions. The bunny nestled inside is quite content, as are those on the side board in front of the early 19th century Regency mirror that hangs in the dining room and is shown on the previous page.

The wonderful stone fireplace warms the family's kitchen. The mantel is home to some antique rabbits flanking blocks that spell out the holiday . . .

The built-in cabinets on either side of the fireplace display a collection of Blue Willow.

This handcrafted farm table, custom made for the homeowners in the Carolinas, invites family and guests alike to gather for and linger over a delicious meal.

COUNTRY KITCHEN

And this sign hanging above the kitchen door, describes the room perfectly - warm and welcoming - full of special touches!

Why bunnies and eggs at Easter?

The egg, symbolizing rebirth and continuing life, and the rabbit, symbolizing fertility, had their roots in spring festivals of ancient cultures long before early Christians viewed the egg as a symbol of the resurrection.

It is thought that the Easter bunny and colored eggs came to our country with German immigrants in the 1700s. They brought their legend of an egg-laying hare who would leave colored eggs as gifts for the children who had been good. Easter candy is a modern addition to our celebrations.

How fortunate for us, our children and grandchildren!

The whimsical hand painted ceramic eggs displayed in the basket on the previous page were crafted by Mrs. Whiteside. Baskets aren't the only way to display eggs. Create an Easter tree. Hand-paint real blown eggs. Add lights and salt dough Easter shapes cut with cookie cutters, baked, and painted. (Recipe can be found in the Appendix.)

Or, create a tree (like the one shown on the opposite page) with tiny bunnies, eggs, birds and other carefully collected ornaments as this Clifton homeowner has done. She actually creates a tree for each season. Her home's new addition is shown in upcoming pages.

Requiring a little more skill, crewel work eggs are nestled in a fresh floral wreath suitable for drying. (Hairspray helps prevent "shedding.") Use year after year. Could change the bunny in the center . . . Lovely!

Create Beautiful Tables

Many of our members are talented floral arrangers. They do it for the artistic satisfaction, for the sheer joy of creating something beautiful for their own homes, and for others to enjoy at special events.

The Paris table at Easter

Bunnies abound at this Easter dessert table – bunnies on the plates and as part of the centerpiece. Creating beautiful tables is one of Mrs. Paris's specialties.

Carnations, Calla Lilies, and Roses,

Peonies and Queen Anne's Lace

Go low or go high . . .

Or alternate . . .

Tulips, Roses, Spider Mums, Stock, and more grace this table below.

Add a little extra to your spring table with napkin folds – a bunny or a bow. (Use a favorite napkin ring with the bow.) More ideas in books & online.

Harmonize Color

Sometimes you might need silks to mix with fresh for color – note the blue accents. It's O.K.

Baskets make perfect containers for flowers, and not just at Easter.

Create Beautiful Dishes, too!

Color is not only important in flower arranging, but in food presentation as well. Making food appealing is an art form that Mrs. Danilchick has perfected. Her food is not only nutritious and delicious, but artfully presented. Her creative flair shows in all she does.

Avocado dip served with fresh raw vegetables

Lightly curried cream sauce topped with breaded chicken cutlet - pomegranates, carrot, lightly steamed spinach, and lightly cooked red cabbage complete the dish.

Mrs. Danilchick's festive Easter table on the following page shows a special Easter cheese, decorated with a cross. In the foreground, lit with candles, are breads iced with confectioners' sugar icing and colorful sprinkles - an Easter treat!

Beautiful table, beautiful food!

More Tempting Spring Treats

TOMATO CUCUMBER AND AVOCADO SALAD

1 ½ c. chopped tomatoes or halved cherry tomatoes
1 c. cucumber, peeled, seeded and diced
1 avocado, sliced
4 oz. cubed feta cheese
2 Tbsp. minced red onion
1 Tbsp. fresh parsley (or 1 tsp. dried parsley)
2 Tbsp. olive oil
1 Tbsp. red wine vinegar
Salt & pepper to taste

Chop tomatoes in medium dice. Add diced cucumber, feta, onion and parsley. Whisk olive oil, red wine vinegar, salt and pepper and pour over salad. Note: Do not slice and add avocado until ready to serve.

CURRIED CHICKEN SALAD

¼ c. low-fat mayonnaise
1 tsp. curry powder
2 tsp. water
1 c. chopped chicken breast (rotisserie is the best)
¾ c. chopped Braeburn apple
1/3 c. diced celery
3 Tbsp. golden raisins
¼ tsp. salt
1/8 tsp. pepper
3 green onions, chopped

Combine mayo, curry, and water in a medium bowl, stirring with a whisk to combine. Add remaining ingredients, stirring well. Cover and chill. Serves 2.

Serve at your beautiful table . . .

. . . Or pack a picnic and enjoy the sunset.

PICNIC CARROT BARS

4 eggs
2 c. sugar
1 c. vegetable oil
3 jars strained baby carrots (2.5 oz.)
2 c. flour
2 tsp. baking soda
1 tsp. salt
1 tsp. cinnamon

Beat eggs and sugar together. Add oil and mix well. Add baby carrots, mix well. Sift together then add: flour, baking soda, salt and cinnamon. Pour into greased jelly roll pan (11" X 15"). Bake at 350 degrees for a metal pan 30-35 minutes; 325 degrees for glass and cool. Frosting: use canned cream cheese frosting or cream together and frost with 4 Tbsp. butter (soft), 3 oz. cream cheese, 1 ½ c powdered sugar and 1 tsp. vanilla.

Picnics are fun in almost any season!

Chapter Three

Summer

Happy Birthday America

Cakes topped with fresh flowers and Marshmallow Rockets!

The Zimmerman Home (seen earlier blanketed in snow) is hidden on a ridge overlooking Castle Creek and nestled between Megills Crossing and Whitehall Farm in historic Clifton, Virginia. The original portion of the home was built in 1868 with two later additions. The original footprint includes a main parlor and two small bedrooms upstairs. The first addition was built in 1953 which is now the office, dining room, and upper level guest room. The second addition was built in 1975 and is the kitchen, laundry room and upper level master bedroom. A detached garage with additional living space was built in 2010.

A three-quarter mile long winding driveway over a small white bridge (shown in the water color in Chapter Four, on page 142) leads to this charming little home.

The interior décor style is described as Country Elegance meets Olde Virginia. There are tall ceilings and large windows throughout. When guests step through the door they are standing on the original 1868 Heart Pine floors.

The office is filled with everyday working items for the Zimmermans' Real Estate Business and family heirlooms, such as Mr. Zimmerman's grandfather's leather football helmet, a family Bible, a Civil War sword, and medals from his own Mountain Climb Summits to name a few.

The Zimmermans' dining room is part of the 1953 home addition. Ten foot ceilings and Mr. Zimmerman's grandmother's dining set are the setting for current day family celebrations with grown children and grandchildren.

The room is painted a beautiful blue which is a lovely contrast to the green space outside the two large windows.

After they purchased the home, the homeowners remodeled the kitchen with creamy white shaker cabinets and dark leather granite counter tops. The kitchen's free-standing cabinet holds many family pieces from Mrs. Zimmerman's grandmothers.

The home's main parlor is where the Zimmermans spend their evenings. The original fireplace is built into the room with bricks to the ceiling. A beautiful new mantel was built to secure the original brick structure. Family antiques and a grandfather clock anchor the room.

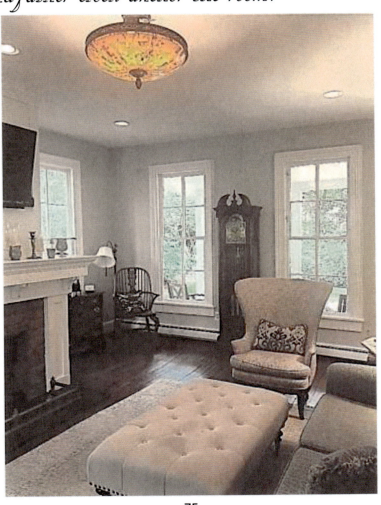

Mirrors make a small space seem larger. These mirrors were collected from antique stores and relatives, then chalk painted and distressed in a deep green. Now they help brighten the stairwell that leads to the second floor.

The original staircase is quite steep but worth the climb. Mrs. Zimmerman had one of the original bedrooms at the top of the stairs converted into her dream closet.

The antique bench, pictured on the next page, was reupholstered and fits this niche in the master bedroom perfectly. The picture above it is of a Civil War era couple in an antique mirror frame. It hung in Mrs. Zimmerman's parents' bedroom when she was a child.

The large master bedroom is a wonderful surprise with an eight foot window over the master bed. Surrounded by trees, it feels like a beautiful sleeping nest.

Another original bedroom is used for guests and grandchildren and holds family antiques and

collectibles like the homeowner's childhood sampler hanging on the wall above the antique chair.

An upper level porch, with access to this large guest bedroom, provides a beautiful view of the seven acre property.

The Zimmermans love to entertain and use their outdoor space for celebrations with family and friends.

The trellis leads from the back porch to the fire pit for year round fun and fellowship. The Zimmerman home is a sweet surprise just outside the town of Clifton, Virginia.

Welcoming Entrances

The driveway to the Esser family's Clifton home is flanked by Bluestone rock pillars. On one side is planted Lucifer's tongue and the other is Spider plant and grasses. The drive leading up to their contemporary home is lined with roses and seasonal flowers.

In the seclusion of the Essers' wooded acreage is the gazebo and kitty pool. (You have to look closely to find the kitties.) A welcome retreat from the summer sun.

The entrance of the Beckman's Fairfax City home is inviting with plants and shrubs lining the graceful curved brick walk. The lovely wreath on the front door awaits guests and says, Welcome, please come in!

... *Welcome to the Beckman home* ...

The furnishings are traditional and beautifully arranged for comfort and conversation. The living room, shown on the opposite page, opens to the dining room where family and friends gather often and enjoy delicious meals.

And there are flowers in every room, including this cozy, relaxing niche – the perfect spot for curling up with a good book in any season!

Perched on a Crystal Quartz and Dolomite base, this exquisite parrot greets visitors to the Joyce home in Fairfax, Virginia. It was purchased in Rio de Janeiro while on a cruise to South America in 2008 – too pretty to resist!

The claws are 18kt gold plated; the eyes are Tiger Eye and Onyx; and the beak is Tiger Eye. The feathers are also a mix of gemstones – some quite rare: Blue Onyx, Sodalite, Yellow Calcite, Serpentinite, Blue Quartz, Rodochrosite, Yellow and White Dolomite, and Jasper.

Not only does this colorful bird provide a welcome greeting to her guests, but for the homeowner, it brings back happy memories of a wonderful vacation she and her husband shared years ago.

Cool Summer Whites

Calla Lilies and Snake plant with a few Hellebores fill a mercury glass candle holder.

Boxwood is tucked into a hat form and topped with a hat adorned with fresh flowers.

And this versatile old basket is filled with Queen Anne's Lace and a candle.

Using stands to vary the height of the containers shown on the previous page, adds interest. Color unifies the grouping.

Blush roses and hydrangeas accented with white Hypericum Berries and Alstromeria grace the coffee table.

White scrim, hung on hooks placed randomly in the ceiling, frames the windows in the guest room. Tulips are a welcome addition to your guest's breakfast tray.

The Swan (Euonymous fortunei 'Interbolwyi') is a beauty in the Leiser family's garden (shown in her arrangements on the previous page). Careful, though – it grows to six to eight feet tall and six to eight feet wide. It blooms from mid-summer through autumn and can be dried for winter arrangements!

The Luchini Great Room

Previously, in the Winter section, we saw the dining room table of this beautiful Clifton home dressed in Tartan Plaid for the holidays. The following pages give us a peak at their family great room and dining room. The massive stone fireplace and hearth is the focal point for this spacious area. Over-sized furniture and rich colors make this a warm place to gather. The large trapezoidal windows reveal the deep woods just outside, and the changing beauty of the seasons.

The Luchinis themselves designed their home, drawing inspiration from old New England "salt box" houses. It was sited to take advantage of the views and was completed in 1990.

The chest shown on the next page is located on the wall to the right of the forward facing sofa.

This painted Asian chest, mirror and antique Rose Mandarin vase stood in a niche in Mrs. Luchini's grandparents' home, and enchanted her as a little girl. When that grandmother was moving to a smaller home, she asked her granddaughter what she would like. Her response: "That corner." Those three pieces remain together to enchant another generation. The carved jade figure, purchased in Singapore, is new, but we think Grandma would approve.

The Luchinis were newly married when they lived in England and filled their home with their favorite antiques, mostly 18th century "Georgian."

The "mule chest" (sideboard) with carved ogee panels, shown on the following page, and Windsor chairs found one by one, are all from this period. The built-in china cabinet (shown on the opposite page) was designed to harmonize with the 18th century English style.

The mid-19th century "girondelles" on top of the mule chest have come down 5 generations on Mrs. Luchini's mother's side. After the original great-great grandmother first displayed them around 1860, they lived in the attic of each succeeding generation, as each in turn found them too "ornate."

Finally this homeowner noticed girondelles in the movie "Gone with the Wind" that looked exactly like hers. She had hers restored, and after 150+ years, they are once again on show in the dining room. They are growing on her.

The centerpiece of the dining room is an Irish Wake Table. The mourners would gather around the deceased whose coffin was placed on this table. After a suitable amount of wailing, the sides came up and the table was laden with food and drink. A grand party sent old Paddy to the hereafter!

Tip: *Think Outside the Vase . . .*

Use fun containers – Ice chest for the wine cellar, with wine corks on wire as accents!

Poker chips for the game room, with playing cards as accents . . .

Hosting a wine tasting? A wooden stirrup adorned with daisies becomes a napkin holder. And what a perfect napkin for the occasion!

How pretty these roses look in this antique gas light fixture on the glass coffee table.

This time this old basket is perfect for the kitchen island filled with veggies, Itea, cabbages and more.

And fresh flowers in a candelabra

with help from this insert and a little oasis.

Who doesn't love red roses in any season!

The Charneco Addition

This new 2024 addition to an already gorgeous Clifton home is faced in stone, matching the stone on the foundation of the original house. It adds a large family room with fireplace, new kitchen with tons of storage, and connects the new kitchen to the garage. Windows abound, making the rooms light and bright.

The other end of the family room shown below, with kitchen just out of sight on left and the dining room entrance center.

Opposite the dining room entrance hall is a more intimate conversation area. Luna, the family's beloved dog, finds the space very relaxing!

The original dining room became an office and powder room, and the old family room was transformed into the beautiful, spacious - yet cozy - dining room with a raised-hearth stone fireplace. Mrs. Charneco's great grandparents' sugar chest, on the wall to the right of the French doors, is just one of her many treasured heirlooms.

What a perfect room for this large family to gather for Sunday dinners!

The chandelier over the dining table came from Puerto Rico via an estate sale. According to Mrs. Charneco, it was in bad shape, but she loved it and had it restored. She describes her taste as "eclectic". She has an eye for combining family pieces with antique and thrift store finds *from around the world. Belle Jar, in Clifton, is a favorite source!*

Their new kitchen is light and bright with plenty of storage. The large island is just the spot for family and friends to gather to keep the cook company. The pendant lights over the island also came from Puerto Rico, but they are antiques from either Spain or Morocco.

Viewed from the family room.

A family piece imbued with memories is this kitchen table, which belonged to her Tennessee grandparents, and then her parents. Remembering her own childhood dinners there, especially Sundays with fried chicken, mashed potatoes, and biscuits, brings her joy.

Perhaps her favorite nook in this remodel is the coffee bar just around the corner to the right of the island.

She enjoys sipping her morning coffee at her grandmother's table while taking in the beauty of the great outdoors.

In closing she writes, "I hope that my home feels warm and inviting and lived in. I think it's important to feel happy in your surroundings."

Summer birthdays? This one was a pirate party. Fold the napkins into boats – which also serve as place cards. Just add a straw for a mast and a paper sail. Black poster board works for the sail and the pirate hat. Shells glued together with a "pearl" center and curly ribbon make the "floral" centerpiece. Cover the table with Kraft paper and put a bucket of crayons at each place to keep guests busy.

The Tastes of Summer –

Cool and fresh or a little spicy.

The Leiser backyard offers a cozy spot for a chilled bowl of Gazpacho or a Baja burger.

GAZPACHO

1-15 oz. can stewed tomatoes
1 medium green pepper, chopped
½ cucumber, diced
1 clove garlic, minced
1 Tbsp. olive oil
1 Tbsp. red wine vinegar
1 tsp. sugar
¼ tsp. Tabasco sauce
Salt & pepper to taste

Combine all ingredients and place in a blender or use an immersion blender. Pulse 6-8 times in order to puree. Chill well.

BAJA TURKEY BURGER

1 lb. lean ground turkey
1 Tbsp. minced seeded jalapeno pepper
¼ c. salsa
1 tsp. minced garlic
½ c. chopped onion
½ tsp. dried oregano
1/8 tsp. salt
1/8 tsp. black pepper

In medium bowl, gently break up turkey. Mix in all remaining ingredients, combining well but do not overmix. Form four burgers and place in freezer for an hour. (This will help the moist burgers stay together when grilled). Spray grill grates or grill pan and cook over medium heat for 5-6 minutes on each side.

Healthy and delicious, plus summer grilling helps keep the kitchen cool!

Chapter Four
Autumn

A chill is in the air . . .

Time to gather around the fire pit...

Or enjoy the visons of fall from the Wood home.

The fall brings brilliant colors into view from the front porch of the Woods Clifton home. The

colors frame the gazebo at the bottom right of the picture. The view epitomizes the beauty of the area surrounding their Victorian farmhouse.

The picture below was taken when the trees were fully leafed, providing nice seclusion with lots of shade in the summer, blooms in the spring, and gorgeous color in the fall. What a difference between the summer view with full foliage and

winter views when the trees are bare . . .
(The Woods say they feel bare, too!)
The couple built their home in 2003, right after the children left the nest – but Mrs. Wood says, "They still found us!"

Nevertheless, it is a delight living close to historic and quaint Clifton. It is definitely home now.

On cool afternoons and pleasant evenings, the Woods often sit in the rockers on the front porch, resting their wine or tea on a Japanese garden stool. Mrs. Wood says her vision is for her porch to welcome visitors with its blue front door and complementary wreath, blue flowers painted by their daughter on the three rockers, and blue outdoor rugs accenting the floor. "We feel fortunate to be able to enjoy and share with each other this view from our porch at this time in our lives."

At the opposite end of the porch is a swing that Mrs. Wood used to soothe her little grandbabies on pretty afternoons when they visited.

Off the living room is the side of their wrap-around front porch. A white bistro table with two chairs overlooks the lavender-fronted gazebo in the back yard. Flat Stanley (a favorite book when their children were growing up) is in the lower right corner and keeps an eye on any activity.

In the background is their gazebo with lights, a fan, music, and maybe a little conversation . . .

"A cocoon protecting us from the hubbub of the world."

The Foyer

Come on in! Mrs. Wood's hope is that the blue wall with her white sculptured flowers scattered on it, warmly welcomes all who enter. These lovely blossoms are her favorite memory of their suite at the Hotel Chateau Monfort in Milan, Italy. She says it was truly the most beautiful,

romantic room in which they have ever stayed. She came home wanting some of that look and feel at her house.

The two pictures on the foyer table are Persian Miniatures (beautiful, delicate inlaid mosaics) from their lives in Tehran showing aged Iranian men typical of those they saw while there.

The two small Cloisonné vases on the table are from China. Mrs. Wood's father brought them back from there when he visited China on business in the late 1970s as the country was reopening to tourists after many years. "I guess we could call it an international tabletop," she says.

Our Red Kitchen!

For Mrs. Wood the color "red signifies life, love, and health – which means "kitchen" to her – thus, the red accent wall, dishes, and the curtains over the sink. Interestingly and inventively, the four curtains are small rugs, cut in half and hung as a "raggy" addition to the décor – why not? I love my kitchen!"

The Persian-Appointed Dining Room

As is often the case, the dining room is right off the front entrance. So, Mrs. Wood thought, "Let's make it pretty!" Her fascination with the color blue continues there, too. Thank goodness there are not many blue foods …

To the back left of the table sits their large Persian samovar. The two pictures framing the China cabinet are Persian paintings of village donkeys carrying their loads and stopping for a drink. Roaming throughout Iran are both donkeys and camels used as beasts of burden.

On holidays, this dining room is filled with family, friends, laughter, companionship, and great food.

The Primary Bath

This is one of Mrs. Wood's favorite picture arrangements in her house: her grandchildren, three boys and one girl, taking bubble baths in her Jacuzzi. Bubbles everywhere! The quote over the tub is "Happiness is a bubble bath." Making it even more special, Mrs. Wood's daughter painted the bubbles on the wall and around the pictures. This picture offers a closer look.

When the photos were taken, the two youngest grandchildren were about four or five and the two oldest were about eight or nine. The pictures were taken over a ten-year period. These kids are now thirteen to twenty-one. Mrs. Wood said that the children's pictures smile at her every time she enters the bathroom.

Twin Guest Bedroom

For one of Mrs. Wood's birthdays, her two children and their spouses surprised her with an antique dress form. She put it in her twin guestroom and dressed it in a roaring twenties outfit she once wore to a party. When guests or grandchildren are staying in that bedroom, she warns them not to be startled during the dark of night by the "Roaring Twenties flapper lady" watching them sleep – yikes!

In front of the window is a "portrait chair" that Mrs. Wood purchased at a neighbor's garage sale. One arm of the chair is high, the other slopes downward. People pose in such chairs for portraits.

The twin beds came from her parents and were brought back from their family's time in Okinawa, Japan. They were Mrs. Wood's and her sister's childhood beds. And now, guests and all her grandchildren have slept in them, too.

Yellow Guest Bedroom

This bright, sunshiny guest room is painted a soft yellow. It's very serene, and one in which it is easy to fall asleep. (Some guests may never leave!)

Mrs. Wood designed and made the wall flower decorations above the bed. Her French phone is on the bedside table, ooh la la …

The Patio

Shortly after moving in, the Woods had a landscape architect add a gazebo, stone patio, dry creek bed, pergola, arbor, and landscape lighting. At one end of the patio is the gazebo. Directly behind the house is the pergola.

At the opposite end is a large circular sitting area surrounding a fire pit. The patio is bordered by a small dry creek bed, which passes under a decorative bridge in the patio. Flower beds are on all sides of the patio – a delight to enjoy throughout the year . . . Beautiful!

As colors fade and autumn draws to a close, thoughts turn to the approaching holidays. The Woods love to celebrate Christmas and their festive decorations delight the neighborhood.

Truly a home for all seasons.

The Colors of

Autumn . . .

Revealed in the splendor of Clifton's own "Clifton Creek"

. . . Inspire Artists!

Watercolor

by

Clifton Artist, Valthea Fry

. . . And make beautiful floral arrangements – oranges, reds, yellows, and rusts with wax flower, grasses, and broom for fillers –

Dried hydrangeas from the garden, silk fall leaves, and a "leafed" craft pumpkin warm the table above. Below, a wreath made from old sheet music holds a small bouquet – maybe for the music room . . .

But, fall colors don't have to be traditional. Magentas are beautiful, too. Perched on a small step stool, they make a dramatic centerpiece for your buffet table.

Halloween Happenings

Fun for kids of all ages!

Yuk! Too much eye of newt!

Halloween is a holiday that again stems from pagan roots. The Celts celebrated Samhain (pronounced SAH-win), a spiritual festival marking the end of summer and where the line between the worlds of the living and the dead blurred. The night before their New Year, (around Nov. 1) people gathered around huge bonfires, dressed in costume so the ghosts would not recognize them, so some say.

As Christianity began to spread, November 1 was designated as a day to honor saints. Since All Saints Day, also known as All Hallows, was observed on November 1, Samhain was eventually called "Allhallows Even" - later shortened to Halloween. Halloween wasn't widely celebrated in the United States until the 19th

century when a large group of Irish and Scottish immigrants arrived and brought with them their customs and traditions.

There are many theories about the origins of Trick or Treating, but it started in this country in the late 1920s and '30s. Cookies, fruit, nuts, coins, and toys were given out. Candy didn't become popular until the 1950s. By the 1970s, wrapped factory-made candy was viewed as the only acceptable treat to hand out on Halloween.

The Irish legend of Stingy Jack may be the source of the Jack-o-Lantern . . . As the story goes, Jack kept trapping the Devil and would let him go only when he promised that Jack would never go to Hell. Alas, when Jack died, Heaven didn't want him, so he was forced to wander as a ghost for all eternity. The Devil gave him a lump of burning coal in a carved out turnip to light his way. So . . . people began carving scary faces in their turnips to scare away "Jack's wandering soul" and other ghosts.

The first carved pumpkins appeared in the U.S. with the Irish immigrants in the mid-1800s. Pumpkins, native to the southwestern United States and northern Mexico, are much easier to carve than turnips!

Halloween is the Pfiffner family's favorite holiday and they go all out. Mr. Pfiffner is the master carver in the family as you can see from his creations on the following page!

Their Burke home welcomes trick-or-treaters of all ages! Enter if you dare . . .

The entrance to the Paris home in Manassas is definitely a treat for trick-or-treaters, too. More awaits inside.

Festive Décor

The Paris kitchen table is set for Halloween.

That's quite a wine glass!

How about carving a watermelon for your Halloween buffet table?

This time the Paris table, ready for a fall luncheon, is shown with colorful napkin rings.

Autumn rushes onward and Thanksgiving is just around the corner. Families gather in homes across the country to enjoy this special American holiday.

The Leiser family's table is ready. The plates are perfect - Botanical Harvest from Pottery Barn - and they look so pretty on the Damask tablecloth with matching napkins! The sterling, Williamsburg Shell by Stieff, completes this festive setting.

The Paris family's table is set, too. Mrs. Paris doesn't always use fresh flowers for her centerpieces. This particular arrangement consists of feathers, grasses, cones and nuts, and maybe a silk leaf or two. Lots of candles at varying heights make her tables very dramatic. And as you've seen, she has dishes for every occasion!

Thanksgiving

The American Thanksgiving holiday is based on a feast the Pilgrims and Wampanoag Indians shared celebrating a rich harvest in the year 1621. President Washington in 1789, urged Americans to set aside a day of thanks, as did every president that followed except for Thomas Jefferson (at the urging of Congress). The actual date to celebrate was left up to the states.

On October 3, 1863, in the midst of the Civil War, Abraham Lincoln proclaimed the national day of "Thanksgiving and praise..." was to be celebrated on November 26, which was the last Thursday in November in 1863.

Thanksgiving was made a paid holiday for Federal workers on January 6, 1885.

While Gimbel's held the first Thanksgiving Day parade in 1920, it is the Macy's Thanksgiving parade, which began in 1924 and was originally called the Christmas Parade, that has become a tradition. Balloons were introduced in 1927 to replace the live animals.

In the late 1930s, wanting to extend the Christmas shopping season to boost the economy, President F. D. Roosevelt tried to establish the 3^{d} Thursday as the day to give thanks, but this was not widely received. Finally in 1942, FDR signed into law the 4th Thursday in November as our national day of thanksgiving.

Today, families across America gather to give thanks, to watch football, and to feast on turkey and all the trimmings – the trimmings often determined by one's family's roots.

Idea: Pinecones and ribbon make simple place cards for this Thanksgiving dinner table. Tuck a strip of paper with your guest's name and add another with a conversation starter in with the "ribbon tail feathers" . . . Might be surprised at what you can learn about your guests.

The Flavors of Fall

PUMPKIN BREAD

2 eggs
1 c. pumpkin puree (Libby's)
½ c. canola oil
1 ¼ c. granulated sugar
¼ c. packed light brown sugar
1 Tbsp. vanilla extract
2 tsp. cinnamon
1 ¼ tsp. ground nutmeg
¾ tsp. ground cloves
¼ tsp. ground ginger
1 ¾ c. all-purpose flour
1 ½ tsp. baking soda
½ c. chopped walnuts, optional

Preheat oven to 350 degrees. Coat a 9" X 5" loaf pan with floured cooking spray or grease and flour.

In a large mixing bowl combine eggs, pumpkin, oil, sugars, vanilla, cinnamon, nutmeg, cloves, and ginger and whisk to combine.

Add flour, baking soda and salt, (if using) and stir until just combined; don't overmix.

Turn batter into prepared pan, smoothing the top lightly with a spatula.

Bake for about 55 minutes or until top is set, domed and a toothpick inserted in center comes out clean or a few moist crumbs. If loaf is browning before center has cooked through, tent with foil for last 15 minutes.

Cool bread in pan for 10-15 minutes before turning out onto a wire rack to cool completely. Store airtight at room temperature for up to 5 days or freeze up to 3 months.

Note: This recipe can be doubled, adding chopped pecans or walnuts to just one loaf. Some cooks like to add 1 c. of mini chocolate pieces.

SHRIMP SCAMPI PASTA

¼ c. olive oil
1 lb. peeled large shrimp
4 garlic cloves, forced through a garlic press
½ tsp. red pepper flakes
½ c. dry white wine
1 tsp. salt
½ tsp. pepper
5 Tbsp. unsalted butter
¼ lb. angel hair pasta
½ c. chopped fresh flat-leaf parsley or 2 Tbsp. dried parsley

Bring 6-8 quart pot of salted water to a boil.
Heat oil in a 12" heavy skillet over moderately high heat until hot but not smoking. Sauté shrimp turning over once until just cooked through, about 2 minutes. Transfer to a large bowl with a slotted spoon. Add garlic, red pepper flakes, wine and salt & pepper in remaining oil, cooking over high heat for one minute. Add butter to skillet, stirring until melted and stir in shrimp. Remove skillet from heat.
Cook pasta in boiling water until just tender, about 3 minutes. Drain pasta, reserving 1 c. of pasta liquid. Toss pasta well with shrimp mixture and parsley in large bowl adding some reserved cooking water if necessary to keep moist.

Note: you can substitute fresh basil leaves, sliced lengthwise for the fresh parsley.

A nice break from poultry in the fall, but definitely delicious in any season!

GRANDMA'S CORN PUDDING

5 large eggs
1/3 c. butter melted and slightly cooled
¼ c. sugar
½ c. milk
¼ c. cornstarch
1-15 oz. can whole kernel corn, drained
2-14 oz. cans cream style corn

Preheat oven to 400 degrees. Grease 2 quart casserole dish. Whisk eggs lightly in large bowl. Add milk, melted butter, sugar and cornstarch. Stir in 3 cans of corn until blended. Pour into prepared casserole. Bake about 1 hour until set in the middle. Serves 8.

This recipe might become a Thanksgiving favorite!

There is so much to be thankful for . . .

Friends and family
Caring neighbors
Good health
Good food
The beauty of our surroundings . . .

A cozy fire . . .

And home . . . home in all seasons.

The Neckels backyard gazebo captures the uniqueness and beauty of each season.

Winter

Spring

Summer

And Autumn

Chapter Five

Retirement Community Living

*Home is where the heart is,
no matter the season,
no matter the size!*

When you enter the Gilbert's spacious apartment in The Woodlands, you are greeted with this lovely view. The living room is comfortable for family gatherings and warm and welcoming for their guests.

The spacious master bedroom with private bath, is just down the hall on the right.

Not seen are the dining room and kitchen which are to the left and the den, and guest room to the right. Downsizing was not easy, but planning ahead was the key. Their cherished treasures surround them.

The balcony affords the perfect spot to continue the homeowner's love of gardening with containers of evergreens and perennials providing year round enjoyment. And it's the perfect spot to sip an early morning cup of coffee.

Using Astilbe, Begonia leaf, and pachysandra, Mrs. Gilbert created this simple but stunning arrangement.

Dr. Kershenstein is very happy with her new apartment and all of the amenities offered at Woodleigh Chase, a brand new retirement community in Fairfax, Virginia.

Outside of her apartment door is a niche which Dr. Kershenstein chooses to decorate for the season or special occasion . . . an extra welcome for her guests.

She feels she has just the space she needs. The guest room complete with sofa bed and desk, also serves as her office.

The living and dining area (not shown) opens onto a balcony, and she has a spacious master bedroom with private bath seen below.

But, perhaps her favorite room might be her brand new kitchen!

While the meals at Woodleigh Chase are delicious, it is nice to have a lovely space to work when you want to stir up a favorite dish or special beverage!

Tip: Try creating a vignette with your arrangements, maybe using some of your cherished mementos, for something a little different.

(Mushrooms are in vogue now!)

The Posts chose Falcons Landing, a continuing care retirement community in Potomac Falls, Virginia for their retirement home. While offered a variety of apartment floor plans as well as a cottage plan with a two-car garage, the Posts

chose a 1630 square foot, two bedroom apartment with den. Large windows make the spacious living area bright and welcoming. It is open to the den on the right, which serves as Mr. Post's office.

This Battalion Flag was presented to Colonel Post at the end of his time in command, 1979-1981. The symbols on it represent all of the battles in which the battalion took part from the Indian Wars through World War Two, to include the Normandy invasion. The Korean chest next to his desk was purchased when he was stationed in Seoul in 1982-83.

The dining area and kitchen are to the right as you enter the apartment.

The Chinese screen was a gift from a family friend who was stationed as an Army Officer in southern China and Burma in the early 1900s. All of the Chinese figures are inlaid ivory, jade, and coral.

The Posts purchased the Chinese chest next to it on a trip to Taiwan when Colonel Post was stationed on Okinawa in 1963-64. It serves as Mrs. Post's silver chest now.

The large master with private bath, not shown, is just off the living room to the left.

The guest room is down the hall to the right. The dolls on the guest bed are Madame Alexander baby dolls ("Puddin" and "Pussy Cat") and belonged to their daughter. In the early 1990s Mrs. Post had them restored. The dollhouse in the corner of the guest room was custom

built for the Posts' daughter in 1971. The artist even signed the bottom of it. By the early 1990s their daughter had graduated from college, launched her career, and married. So, Mrs. Post became the benefactor of the doll house! She found a wonderful doll house shop in Vienna, Virginia, and over the next ten years the shop proprietor electrified the house, wall papered the rooms and sold her beautiful doll house furniture! The curtains were made by a lady on his staff out of Colonel Post's great aunt's lace handkerchiefs. It is now a treasured "heirloom" . . .

The Smiths chose The Woodlands, located in Fairfax County Virginia, for their retirement home. They had been members of the Clifton community for over 50 years when they downsized. Mrs. Smith is a charter member of CCWC. She was also a former garden club

member. Maybe the beautiful arrangement on the coffee table gave her away.

The living room in their new apartment reflects the couples' exquisite taste, knowledge and appreciation of antiques, and love of color. They have plenty of room for entertaining their family and friends, and make all who visit feel most welcome.

The Woodlands offer residents many activities from which to choose - interesting speakers, excursions to community events, holiday celebrations, not to mention various activity groups in which one can take part. But every now and then, it is nice to just stay home - maybe work a puzzle.

Looks like they may have one underway. . .

Chapter Six

CCWC

What We Do

CCWC Beginnings

Charter member, Diane Smith

The Clifton Community Woman's Club, or CCWC as it is more commonly known, was formed in 1971 as part of the General Federation of Women's Clubs. Its founder was Kitty Bean who had been a member of the Falls Church Woman's Club until she moved with her family to Clifton. At that time Clifton was a very rural area in Fairfax County, Virginia. The small incorporated town had not attracted any new people, and the amenities were few. Most homes had "pit privies" until the County installed a "pump and haul" system which allowed for some limited growth in town.

Into that venue came a number of young families who had moved to the Washington, DC area and had settled in Fairfax County. Most of them had young children, worked for some form of the Federal Government, and were looking to settle in a less busy area. Kitty was able to gather 31 women to be charter members of CCWC. She was able to do this in part because several groups had already formed to oppose a county waste station proposed for the Fairfax Station area, and a large regional airport proposed for the same area. The opposition to both of these was great, and Kitty was able to channel that passion into the Woman's Club.

The General Federation of Women's Clubs is an international organization with a mostly philanthropic purpose, and as with many philanthropic organizations, there is an expectation to pay dues and support their fundraising. In 1972 a member suggested that CCWC put on a Home's Tour to raise funds, and the rest as they say, is history. The Homes Tour grew in popularity, and was able to fund scholarships for high school and college students for many years. Covid caused a five-year interruption in the tours, but with the support of our sponsors and new programs, such as Speakers for Scholarships, CCWC has been able to maintain its charitable funding. The Homes Tour will be reinstated in 2025.

Programs and Committees

The objective of the Clifton Community Woman's Club is to serve the community through activities and projects that enhance the cultural, educational, and physical well-being of the community, and to support the objectives and programs of the General Federation of Women's Clubs and its affiliates.

Community Service Programs

Arts and Culture – promotes appreciation of the Arts
Creative Arts – recognizes members' achievements at the annual spring Arts and Crafts Contest.
Environment – encourages members' awareness
Education and Libraries
Scholarships, Bridge Club, Bunco, Book Club
Health and Wellness
Community Support, Helping Hands, Food For Others, Lamb Center Lunches
Citizen Engagement and Outreach
Great Decisions, Awareness of Public Issues

Standing Committees

Awards
Budget and Finance
Charitable Contributions
Communications -
Newsletter, Yearbook, Webmaster, Facebook
Federation Reports – prepares annual reports
Helping Hands – assists members in need, food etc.
Hospitality – arranges for refreshments at meetings
Membership
Ways and Means – organizes fundraising activities
Clifton Day – annual community event in which we participate

The Lamb Center

Karen Kershenstein

CCWC has been providing lunches at the Lamb Center on the second Monday of the month since June 2018. CCWC also supports the Lamb Center annually through its charitable giving program.

The Lamb Center is a daytime drop-in shelter for individuals who are experiencing homelessness in Fairfax County, Virginia. The Center provides guests with breakfast, lunch, showers, laundry service, Bible studies, case management, employment opportunities, housing and job counseling, AA meetings, small group opportunities, nurse practitioner services, a dental clinic, and much more.

As a Christian ecumenical community of faith, the Lamb Center works on behalf of all people experiencing poverty or homelessness regardless of race, religion, creed, or any other status, and strives to provide a safe and welcoming space, honoring each individual's dignity and experience. It also collaborates with community members, businesses, local governments, and faith communities to discover solutions that equip guests not just to survive but, more importantly, to thrive.

The Lamb Center is in the early stages of building a facility that will provide permanent supportive housing to as many as 55 homeless individuals. It has purchased property for the facility, and construction is expected to begin in 2025.

Scholarships
Barbara Keller

Each year the CCWC raises funds to provide four scholarships to students attending George Mason University, Northern Virginia Community College, and a local high school that is selected annually. The George Mason University School of Performing Arts receives one scholarship every year and an additional school at the University is selected each year to receive a second scholarship. Northern Virginia Community College and the selected high school receive one scholarship each. CCWC raised enough funds this year to be able to fund the scholarships at $2,000 each.

****

In addition to scholarships, our contributions to other charitable organizations make an impact on our community. Below are just a few quotes from the many notes of appreciation we have received over the years.

Scholarship recipient: "I'm incredibly grateful to the Clifton Community Woman's Club for this wonderful opportunity as recipient of the GMU Science Scholarship. Your support motivates me to strive for excellence and make an impact in healthcare and beyond."

Principal of Brookfield Elementary: "Your contribution will be added to our emergency fund to help support our students in need."

Executive Director of Cloverleaf Equine Center: "Thank you for being such faithful supporters of Cloverleaf and our mission!"

Executive director of National Alliance on Mental Illness: "Our most humble thanks for your continued generosity to our mission."

Environment Committee Tips

Vickie Luchini

The Environment Committee, previously known as Conservation and Gardening, promotes awareness of local resources, conservation issues, and interest in the beautification of our community. The committee sponsors gardening demonstrations, coordinates visits to local gardening points of interest, provides floral support for various club projects, and writes articles/tips for our monthly Newsletter.

Eco-Tip: As much as possible, create a TREE-FREE HOME in all seasons.

- Replace paper napkins with cloth napkins – if each family member gets a different color you don't have to wash after each use.
- Replace paper towels with cloth towels and just wash and reuse.
- If you print documents, print on once-used paper and/or bleach-free, recycled paper with the highest post-consumer waste content available.
- Switch to a digital organizer for tracking your to-do's and grocery lists. A few free suggestions: Wunderlist, Remember the Milk, todolist.
- Reuse envelopes, wrapping paper, the front of gift cards (as postcards) and other paper materials you receive wherever possible.
- Read books, magazines, and newspapers from your local library or online.
- Create and use note pads from once-used paper.
- Leave messages for family members on a reusable message board.

Eco-Tip: Conserve Water
- Fix leaking pipes and insulate.
- Keep the running tap closed while you brush your teeth.
- Recycle water in your home.
- Use water-saving appliances.
- Collect rainwater in a rain barrel to water your lawn.
- Shorten your shower time.
- Keep water in a jug in the fridge.
- Wash full loads in washing machine and dishwasher.
- Mulch plants to retain moisture.

If you are going out to eat and might take home leftovers, bring your own container. Experts differ on how long it takes that Styrofoam box to decompose. The answers range from 500 years to NEVER!

In season, shop your local Farmers' Markets!

Tip: Go "Green" with Gold – Peggy Cranston

Most of us have things around the house in need of a pick-me-up. Try leafing instead of painting. Metal leaf can be found in most craft stores. It is not difficult to work with and can make a huge difference in an old piece of furniture, a lamp, or an old frame. And, it keeps them out of the dump which is definitely good for the environment! Embellish with an old piece of jewelry or "out-of-fashion" button cover.

For a more "antique" look, the middle frame, pictured below, has separated embroidery strands glued in bunches to the frame before leafing. Then a glaze of thinned burnt umber was added to tone down the gold.

The glass vase behind the center frame was gold leafed using painters tape to define the stripes. Leaf where the tape isn't; then remove the tape!

Transform a worn bathroom cabinet. Mix gold and silver leaf for a softer and more interesting look. Apply the leaf sheets randomly, but cover the old surface completely. Then, leaf a large frame and hang it over the builders' grade mirror above the cabinet for a new look at very little cost. Seal with a sealant.

Appendix
2024-25 Sponsors of
Clifton Community Woman's Club

Angela Ganey
Belle Jar Design, Kerry Powers, Owner *
Clifton Lions Club *
Democratic Women of Clifton and Northern Virginia *
Diane and David Smith
Dianne and Ken Whiteside
Eminence Jewelers
Fairfax Station Railroad Museum
Friends of the Burke Centre Library
GMU Performing Arts Center *
Integrated Sports Medicine & Physical Therapy *
Interstate Worldwide Relocation Services *
Jennifer C. H. Diaz, DMD, MS, Periodontics and Implant Dentistry*
JL Tree Service
Kathleen and Jack Mayer
Kay and John Gilbert
Megan Pfiffner Nutrition *
Morrissette Family Foundation
Northern Virginia Electric Coop NOVEC *
Priscilla Moore, ReMax Allegiance *
Republican Women of Clifton
Senator Stella G. Pekarsky
The Leiser Family
The Woodlands Retirement Community
Trish and Evans Mandes
Valerie and Ron White
Westlands Dental, Dr. Jarrell

*Our eBook Sponsors
https://cliftoncwc.org/preferred-business-sources-ebook/

Credits/Contributors

Denna Zimmerman, Jan Wood, Sue Witton, Dianne Whiteside, Diane Smith, Ida Portland, Joyce Post, Karen Paris, Vickie Luchini, Charlene Leiser, Karen Kershenstein, Barbara Keller, Shirley Joyce, Kay Gilbert, Helen Esser, Tanya Danilchick, Dianne Charneco, Peggy Cranston, Linda Beckman, Sylvia Auton

Seasonal Recipes provided by Linda Beckman

Image Credits

Members of the Clifton Community Woman's Club, and Patti Ballinger, Dianne Charneco, Irina Cranston, and Jim Wood

Editors

Sue Adams, Peggy Cranston, and Vickie Luchini

Floral Design

The Clifton Community Woman's Club Flower Committee: Dianne Whiteside, Joyce Post, Joanne Neckel, Janet Micari, Vickie Luchini, Charlene Leiser, Kay Gilbert, Sandy Dunn, Tanya Danilchick, and Peggy Cranston

Sheet Music Wreath created by Nancy Marshall

Cover Design

Peggy Cranston

Home Owners:

Members of the Clifton Community Woman's Club and Dianne Charneco

Recipe for Salt Dough Shapes

Supplies:

Rolling pin
Ruler
Easter cookie cutters – or appropriate cutters for other holidays
Spatula
Straw to make holes
Parchment paper to cover cookie sheets
Acrylic paint
Sealer/polyurethane
Ribbon/cord/ fish line

Recipe:

Preheat oven to 250 degrees
Cover baking sheets with parchment paper
Mix and knead, 1 cup flour, ½ cup salt, 1/3 cup water
Roll to ¼ inch thick
Cut shapes with cutters and put on baking sheets
Make a hole for hanging
Bake at 250 for 2 hours
Cool and paint with acrylics – apply sealer
Add ribbon for hanging

Spray a tree branch and secure in container with pebbles, marbles, etc.

Add lights if desired and hang your creations!

This recipe was used to make some of the items on the Easter tree seen on page 50.

Whether social or charitable, all of our activities promote Friendships

In all seasons!

About the Authors – the CCWC Membership

CCWC celebrated their 50th anniversary in 2021. The two ladies in front with corsages are charter members – left to right, Betty Boyd and Diane Smith. Betty Boyd has since passed away, but was a faithful, active member for 50 years. Others on the front row are past members and invited guests.

CCWC members are caring ladies from all walks of life – nurses, teachers, IT experts, scientists, authors, artists, travel agents, real estate agents, homemakers, government workers, Yoga instructors, and more. Some have lived and traveled all over the world. All are interested in helping those in need. All love their homes and their communities.

The CCWC has done much over the last 50 plus years to make a difference in our communities – to be good stewards of the environment – to provide for those who are in need of food, clothing, mentoring, and scholarships. Members have sent letters to service men and women, supported local schools in need, local food banks, and local shelters – have made hats for cancer patients, and dresses for children in Africa so they could go to school. The needs are great. The money raised from your purchase of this book goes into CCWC's Charitable Trust Fund to support these efforts. CCWC is truly grateful for your support. Thank you.

Make a House a Home

It takes a lot of things,
to make a house a home.
To make a place of comfort,
out of wood and wire and stone.
It takes photographs and souvenirs,
and knickknacks on the shelves.
Memories of ones we love
and pieces of ourselves.
It's flowers planted by the door,
and dinner on the stove.
The kind of life lived down to earth,
with guidance from above.
But, exactly what it takes the most
is kindness that is shown,
By people and the love they spend,
to make a house a home.

From Peter Townsends Irish Blessings